For my little cousins Joseph, Cora, Stanley, Isla,
Libby, Leo, Alice and Annie – MH

In loving memory of Malak xx – RA

Inspiring | Educating | Creating | Entertaining

Brimming with creative inspiration, how-to projects, and useful
information to enrich your everyday life, Quarto Knows is a favourite
destination for those pursuing their interests and passions. Visit our
site and dig deeper with our books into your area of interest:
Quarto Creates, Quarto Cooks, Quarto Homes, Quarto Lives,
Quarto Drives, Quarto Explores, Quarto Gifts, or Quarto Kids.

With thanks to the following schools where children gave us their suggestions:
Bruce Grove Primary in London; Edith Moorhouse School in Carterton;
St Barnabas School in Oxford and
St George's International School in Luxembourg.

Text © 2018 Mary Hoffman. Illustrations © 2018 Ros Asquith.

First published in 2018 by Frances Lincoln Children's Books, an imprint of The Quarto Group
The Old Brewery, 6 Blundell Street, London N7 9BH, United Kingdom.
T (0)20 7700 6700 F (0)20 7700 8066

www.QuartoKnows.com

A catalogue record for this book is available from the British Library.

ISBN 978-1-78603-054-2

The illustrations were created with watercolours
Set in Green

Published by Rachel Williams
Designed by Judith Escreet
Edited by Katie Cotton and Kate Davies
Production by Kate O'Riordan

Manufactured in Dongguan, China [TL]
9 8 7 6 5 4 3 2 1

MIX
Paper from
responsible sources
FSC® C104723

The Great Big Book of Friends

Can you find ME every time you turn a page?

Mary Hoffman and Ros Asquith

Frances Lincoln
Children's Books

What is a Friend?

What do you think a friend is?

FRIENDS ARE LIKE FAMILY

Hi there!

MAKING friends

We've got the same book!

Some people find it easier to make friends than others do.

Hello!

This is Horatio Ponsoby-Bartholomew.
He likes drawing frogs, too.

How do you DO that?

I like you!

You're clever.

Do you remember how you made all your friends?
It might have been at school or playgroup
or at a party.

We've got the same name!

What team do you support?

Do you like cats?

What's your name?

You have to be a bit brave sometimes
to ask to be someone's friend.

We can feel a bit lonely if we think
we don't have any friends. But it's
OK to be on your own sometimes.

Do you have one person who is your best friend?

Our parents were best friends.

We were best friends at nursery.

And we're STILL best friends!

If we have babies, will THEY be best friends?

Who Knows?

How do you know if someone is your best friend?
Maybe it's the person you most like to do things with. . .

the one who is best at
cheering you up. . .

and the one you feel
comfortable with,
just being together.

You don't have
to pretend. . .

Cos I'm your
best friend.

My best friend
feeds me.

What if you don't have just one special friend? You might prefer to have more.

I'd like a group of friends, please.

BEST PRICE ON BULK BUY

That group looks more fun than my group.

It can be a lot of fun doing things with a group of friends, playing games and talking about things you all enjoy.

Friendship groups can last a lifetime, till you are all grown up and maybe have children of your own.

They're overtired.

You sometimes see groups of grown-ups having fun together and being silly, just the same way they did when they were kids.

Family or Friends?

Great-Aunty

second mum

step mum

step dad

'half-brother'

'Nearly sister'

Have you got a brother or sister? When you are very young, you might not think of them as friends but as you get older they can be the very best kind. And they've known you longer than anyone else.

My little brother was useless.

Then he was annoying.

Now he's my best friend.

Brother Sister Uncle Aunt

Grandpa Mum

The same can be true of cousins or maybe your grandparents.

GRANDPA is my BEST FRIEND.

But if you are an only child or you don't get on well with your brothers and sisters, your friends can become like family.

Kittens leave home at eight weeks old – can't wait!

Great-uncle   Great-Grandma   GRANDMOTHER   Great-Grandfather   Mum   Dad

Dad DADDY Mother Father Mummy   step mum

WE SHARE JOKES.

SHARING

We share sweets.

We share UMBRELLAS

we share a BATH.

Quite often we become friends with someone else because of sharing something.

No! You can't share the CAT's food.

We SHARE COMICS

It might be when we are quite little and someone holds a toy out to us or it might be later when we discover we enjoy the same food, games, music or books.

We SHARE POOLS

We have so much in common.

WE SHARE CLOTHES.

we share Books.

we share playgrounds

we share food.

we share toys.

We can share secrets
with our friends too.

Sharing space can be tricky . . .

Friendship often seems to be
about sharing. As we get older
we might share ideas and
opinions rather than things.

we share beds

we share paints

BEING DIFFERENT

We aren't only friends with people who are just like us. Sometimes it's great to have friends who are quite different from us, and who like different things.

Why not write down things you both have in common?

We have **NOTHING** in common.

We both have
A head.
A body.
Teeth.
We both like CAKE.
We are both PEOPLE!

CATS ARE DIFFERENT TOO.

They can help us learn about new ideas or inspire us to try new activities.

A FRIEND you haven't MET

Have you met all your friends? It might sound like a strange question, but it is possible to be friends with someone you have never met.

I've got friends all over the world!

Hallo vinur!

רבח יה

Helo, ffrind

Ciao amico!

Hello friend!

嘿，朋友

Hei venn

привет друг   ¡Hola amigo!   hello aboki

Salut l'ami!

Ahoj kamarát

Hallo Freund!

Sawubona friend!

You may have a pen pal who lives in another country and you can stay in touch by writing emails and letters.

친구야, 안녕

Do you have a friend that only you can see? That's a very special kind of friend that not everyone has.

Happy Birthday!

Imaginary friends can be boys or girls, animals or fantastic creatures. They are always there when you need someone to talk to or to play with.

I need two ice creams. One is for Foo-Foo.

THING

(Thing has springs, wings & sings)

SCRUFFY

Half boy, half tomato plant

MRS FLIPPY

Half beetle half fish

MR PIGGY RIDER

HE RIDES PIGS!!

OUR INVISIBLE FRIENDS

Sometimes you can say that they're the ones who have broken something or done something naughty when really it was you. And they never seem to mind.

ANIMAL friends

For quite a lot of people their pet is their friend.
A dog is always pleased to see you.

Cats know when you are upset and come to comfort you. And stroking an animal can make you feel calm and happy. No wonder we talk about our "furry friends."

But some great pets aren't furry at all!

Sorry, but NITS are NOT pets.

Can a fish be a friend?

Animals can be friends with each other too.

I'll be your friend, as long as I don't have to eat lettuce.

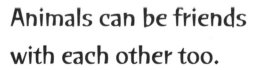

Sometimes a friend may not be a person at all.

We all have days when a teddy or a special blanket or a story feel more friendly to us than our actual friends do. But that's okay.

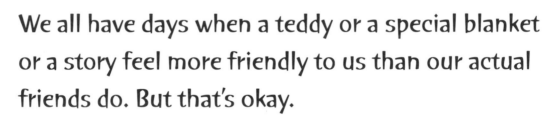

A cat's best friend is a laundry basket.

And a familiar book can always cheer us up.

A lot of friendship is about comfort, familiarity and just being there when needed.

When Friends FALL OUT

Even the very best friends can have arguments – which isn't surprising, because they're the ones you spend the most time with. You might fall out and think you don't want to be friends any more.

It's a horrible feeling when you think
your friend has stopped liking you.

But good friends can usually get over
their quarrels and make things up.
Sometimes it takes a week – or you
might be friends again by lunch.

 LOSING friends

You can lose a friend even when you don't want to. Because it's the grown-ups who make most of the decisions in life, your very closest friend might have to go and live somewhere very far away so that you hardly ever see them.

Their parents might have to go abroad for work.

Or their parents might decide they should go to another school. It's really hard to stay friends with someone when you don't see them every day and you know they are making new friends.

It's sad to be the one left behind, but you will make new friends yourself too.

Who is **NOT** your friend?

There are some people who are just never going to be your friends. For whatever reason, you don't like them and they don't like you.

But you might still have to spend time with them every day, if they are in your class at school or live near to you.

It's better if you can find a way to get along with them. You don't have to be close friends with anyone you don't like but you really don't want to have enemies. And you might be surprised – someone you don't like at first may become a good friend.

HOW MANY friends?

How many friends have you got? Just one, or too many to count? Or do you feel that you haven't got any real friends? That can be a lonely feeling. But you don't have to be with friends to have a good time.

Mum Dad FISHY

I got 3 friends.

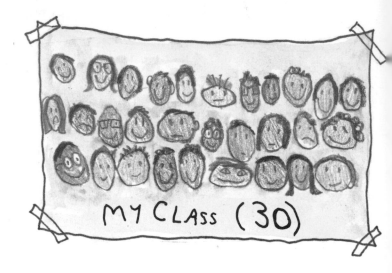

MY CLASS (30)

ONE friend NEXT doOR

The older you get, the more people you will meet and the more friends you will make – and if you never stop being friends with any of them you might end up with a large number. There's no right number of friends to have and it's fine not to have any.

Friends Forever

Look around at the friends you have. It may be hard to imagine now, but one day you will look back on all being kids together and laugh over the funny things you did when you were little.

It's good to think you might still know some of them when you are grown up, isn't it?